Temptations For A Juvenile Delinquent

Sky Gilbert

ECW PRESS

MISFIT

Published by ECW PRESS
2120 Queen Street East, Suite 200, Toronto, Ontario, Canada M4E 1E2

NATIONAL LIBRARY OF CANADA CATALOGUING IN PUBLICATION DATA

Gilbert, Sky
Temptations for a juvenile delinquent / Sky Gilbert.

Poems.
a misFit book

ISBN 1-55022-612-6

I. Title.

PS8563.I4743T43 2003 C811'.54 C2003-902190-4
PR9199.3.G5248T43 2003

Editor: Michael Holmes / a misFit book
Cover and Text Design: Darren Holmes
Cover Art and Author Photo: David Hawe
Production and Typesetting: Mary Bowness
Printing: Marc Veilleux Imprimeur Inc.

This book is set in Bembo and Imperial

The publication of *Temptations For A Juvenile Delinquent* has been generously supported by the Canada Council, the Ontario Arts Council, and the Government of Canada through the Book Publishing Industry Development Program. Canadä

DISTRIBUTION
CANADA: Jaguar Book Group, 100 Armstrong Avenue, Georgetown, ON L7G 5S4

UNITED STATES: Independent Publishers Group, 814 North Franklin Street, Chicago, Illinois 60610

PRINTED AND BOUND IN CANADA

ECW PRESS
ecwpress.com

it’s all for Ian, really

APPETIZERS

DELINQUENT POEMS

FAIRY TALES

TO THE ONE I LOVE

FROM "WHAT LITTLE TRUTHS WE KNOW FOR SURE ABOUT THE LIFE AND TIMES OF CASPER G. SCHMIDT"

WORLD WEARY

DESSERT

APPETIZERS

The Book Women

they came by the hundreds
they came by the thousands
they came in caftans
they came in San Salvadoran ponchos
they came in smart sweater sets
they came wearing tri-coloured spectacles
they came with pussy willows in their hair
they are the book women
heavy browed and heavy breasted
they approach me
after my reading
they talk of my sensitivity
"is it because you're gay?" they ask
indeed I dare not say for certain
but instead, suggest —
"there must be sensitive straight men in the world, too"
The Book Women look at me skeptically
when I make this assertion
and then then they talk of David Leavitt
"don't you just love his novels?"
actually, I detest them
but instead, I say —
"he's unputdownable, eh?"
then The Book Women ask me
the twelve million dollar question
"aren't you just trying to say that we're all,
well, basically the same, inside?"
that's not exactly what I'm trying to say
but I lie
you have to lie to The Book Women
because soon they must return to their cold
bloated, red-faced workaholic husbands
to affluence without influence
and a society which carelessly tosses them aside

because they are old
you must lie to The Book Women
because inside, we are all Book Women
and though some of us may have larger breasts
or more colourful ponchos
we are all in danger of going mad
Ophelia-like
our hair stuffed with pussywillows
our heavy caftans weighing us down
like regrets
buried each in the raging waves
of our own delusional seas

Winnipeg Farts
(for Ian)

no one farts in Winnipeg
it would wake the geese
only toques can make you happy
and the bathroom floor is heated
everything goes on forever
until you get to the end

then it stops

I want you to love me desperately
but please don't do it in Winnipeg
you promise, don't you?
I saw a boy in Winnipeg
his arms were soft and hairy
I listened to some music in Winnipeg
but nothing could pierce the vast grey sky
that painting belonged to my grandmother!
and the people are so friendly
or so they say, but still —
it's Louis Riel you long for —
and you understand why their Puritan passion
just had to wrench the life out of him
(one imagines he had erections, after all
like any Frenchman)

the next time I go down on you honey
will you make me forget I ever went to Winnipeg?

I farted quite publicly in Winnipeg
and no one seemed to notice

but somewhere far off in the lonely forest a bird died
such is the power of wishing and wanting and wallowing

in a place where even despair is muted
by wheat

yet beige is not my colour

do your eyes still sparkle, in spite of Winnipeg?
when can I see them again, my darling?

oh when can we wear pajamas
and jump up and down on feathery beds
make stains, and celebrate our bodily functions?
not in sunny Manitoba, please
far far far from The Prayeree

Ten Reasons I'm Frightened

"There ain't no lady goin' to break my heart, as long as I have my horse!"
— Gene Autry

1. Everyday I get older.
2. You're smarter than me.
3. I'm avoiding mirrors.
4. You seem to like my belly.
5. Arthritis seems, well, normal.
6. You seem like a very very very awfully nice guy.
7. I needn't go out tonight. Really, I might as well not. I could just sit at home and watch TV.
8. You're absolutely beautiful, enough.
9. I don't know how to dance to that music; there's no tune.
10. This could be the one, this could be it, so everything would stop, I would no longer go out, fuck, be crazy, come home drunk, listen to Victorian operettas, have anxiety attacks, buy vicious cats, eat too much, do poppers, suck in my cheeks, diet, smoke, worry, jerk off, be very afraid, wait for my favorite box of cheese crackers from my Dad in the mail, have a love/hate relationship with my own body, fantasize about moving to New York, get strange letters from cute boys, wear revealing clothes, get pierced, fart in bed at night, feel guilty . . . or hope. . . .

DELINQUENT POEMS

In Defense of J.D.

Which stands for juvenile delinquent. I can't understand why they keep asking why. The world is cruel. Especially people. And Holden wants to catch them before they, you know, fall off the world. And can't you see that this guy just can't hack it? I mean, the worst thing is to be like a friend of Hemingway's and everything. To be convinced you are a serious writer and then to be told you're not. You're thirty years old for Chrissakes and *The New Yorker* is just starting to take you seriously and then the critics start saying you're sentimental and it's just because people are buying your books, basically. Even though you are sentimental. Shit, that's just too much disappointment — it really is. Can't they understand? Are they stupid, or just so phony that they don't even know what it's like to have dreams?

And it really pisses me off that some damn book I read said that *The Catcher in the Rye* was found in the back pocket of the guy who shot Lennon, and the guy who shot Reagan, and the one that shot that What's-Her-Name-Starlet. Does that make it some sort of fucking assassin's primer? Jesus, just think for a minute. Could it just be the most popular book in the world, in every other kid's pocket? And not just the pockets of the crazy guys? Sometimes I wish you people would think for a minute before you open up your stupid mouths.

And then there's all this innuendo, all this stuff, about him liking little girls. Well so what? Did the guy ever actually molest anybody? I don't think so. If you can't prove it then why don't you just shut up? Maybe sometimes he had bad taste in little girls, like that Maynard character who got breast implants when she grew up. Breast implants for fuck's sake! We live in this whole culture based on family and loving children, but if some guy loves children too much — I don't even want to get into it. It's sickening what you're implying about him. And even if he does want to fuck teenage girls now and then, Jesus Christ, who doesn't? I'm gay and even *I* find them sexy sometimes. Teenage girls are fucking sexy and they know it.

But the main thing is this: juvenile delinquents never grow up. Not the real ones anyway. And this Salinger guy, the one thing he isn't, is phony.

The Butterfly Academy

The butterfly academy
nurtures and trains young butterflies.
Here, there are no football teams, gym classes,
or fat, scary, bespectacled special education teachers
named Mrs. Nerve.
No.
Instead, mornings are devoted to fluttering,
afternoons to picking the prettiest flowers to rest upon,
while evenings, of course, are all about being beautiful.
And for the boy who dares to whisper to his mother,
"When I grow up, I want to be a butterfly!"
there is no shock, jeering, worry —
for tuition, as we know, is always free.

Coming Out

When I was 28 I attended a men's group for homosexuals and bisexuals concerned with the trials and tribulations of living in a heterosexual society in which we discussed (among other things) the strains and stresses of being male and somehow not, and the pressures and ramifications of our socio-political choices, all in a wide cultural yet totally personal context. Through our frank and comprehensive group interactions we hoped to free ourselves and relax, but also to analyze and dissect the warp and the woof of our psychological and social mores, the morass and moraine of our inner emotional and spiritual terrain. It was, in fact, an exercise in contrasting dualisms, an exploration of the male and female, heterosexual and homosexual, aggressive and passive forces within — double, two, binary, twin.

And during some of these discussions — always so tense yet trembling with the possibility of release, so terrifying and yet so strangely reassuring — I happened to glance out of the rear window of the third storey flat where these meetings took place.

Below me stretched a vast uncharted forest (a jungle really) dark and deep, verdant and lush, where a dense green valley plunged precipitously to a cleansing stream, overhung with fragrant, swaying vines. The cries of exotic birds pierced the air as they soared from tree to tree, occasionally lighting to spread their beautiful feathers in an obscene, erotic display.

A couple of years after that I became a homosexual.

I quit the men's group, no longer having a need for it.

I returned to the house.

(It was located on a moderately busy residential street.)

I walked behind the house.

I searched for the jungle, the verdant valley, the cleansing stream.

I found a solitary tree.

Recipe for Living with a Troubled Teen

There are the Terrible Twos
and the even more Terrifying Threes
and before you know it,
you'll find yourself living with
a Troubled Teen.
Here are some handy tips.

1. When his door is shut
there is to be no discussion,
he wishes to be alone.
Certainly you may wonder, and worry.
How you might wish to pluck up your courage and knock!
A little "Hello" or "What's on your mind, honey?"
might seem like
a cheery,
practical way to initiate conversation.
But no,
for the Troubled Teen, these forays,
however well intentioned,
will seem like nothing less than a vile,
unwarranted intrusion,
an ambush, an arrest.
Best to let him stew in his own juice
until he ventures out of his own accord.
Have patience.
Eventually you will hear the perky ping of the microwave
or smell the somewhat unwelcome fragrance
of a gooey Kraft Dinner.
And you can rest content with the knowledge
that your Troubled Teen,
in need of simple nourishment,
has stirred from his lair,
ready to visit the civilized world.

2. Even then
it's best not to jump him
with a flurry of prying questions.
Remember, even a look of loving concern
may be misinterpreted.
But if you wait for your Troubled Teen to come to you
the rewards may be greater than you had ever imagined.

3. Respect his moods, his inedible foods,
his frustrating toilet habits,
the mysterious hairs in the sink
and the phone numbers scribbled on the back
of the hydro bill.
Do not discard anything.
I repeat, do not discard anything.
Leave his clothes where he dropped them
and never move them without his permission.

4. When he steals for you
— and he will —
accept the illicit plunder gratefully,
neglecting to inquire from whence it came.
And if your Troubled Teen asks you to steal with him
remember that
the family that plays together
stays together.
So in the spirit of *Breakfast at Tiffany's*
why not, after all, join in?

5. Of course the time will come
when your Troubled Teen will ask you to partake of his drugs.
It's always best to answer "Yes."
Even if, after partaking,
you find yourself spread-eagled and tied
to the livingroom couch.
Remember, it's the least you can do for him.
And for yourself.

All in all, the rewards of living
with a Troubled Teen far outweigh
the fleeting moments of frustration and discouragement.
Perhaps you may find yourself, years later, yearning
for those heady days to return.
But if you follow this simple, healthy recipe,
you and your Troubled Teen
will spend many happy hours together,
and you may very well make from lemons
that are both old and under-ripe
a lovely lemonade,
and from over-fresh eggs and slightly rancid vinegar,
a tart and tantalizing mayonnaise.

Something Else

in my dream I keep visiting different rooms
of a very large hippie household
it's miles from the ghetto
(how will I ever get home after the bars?)
some of the apartments are spacious and homey
I can wander around the crumbling, capacious halls
my straight neighbors are rarely if ever home
or they're vicious
the landlord is some sort of cheat
some of the apartments are very dark and dirty
there is a communal kitchen
suspicious substances stuck to an old pan
should I move there?
or should I stay in my tiny apartment
so comfortable in the heart of my own gay community?
in my dream I waver, back and forth
visiting one apartment and then the other
and then I meet Cavafy
who is lounging in a chair, his shirt unbuttoned
every inch the satisfied Daddy
and he curls his finger and beckons me to his side
"you needn't live above a brothel, even though I do"
I love everything about him
especially his charming Greek/Brit accent
"you needn't live above a brothel,
as long as you have a brothel in your mind"
at that point, a naked young man, wet from the shower, wanders
carelessly into the livingroom, toweling his hair
"although actual proximity has its advantages"
Cavafy and the boy don't touch each other
and for a moment I wonder, is it because they already have?
or is it something else

Letters from Verlaine to Rimbaud

1. I don't know what you dream of
but the way you thrash around at night frightens me
the cat hides and the candle sputters
and in the morning you are a wet mess of tangled sheets
what tortures you?
why?
if that stupid good-for-nothing
farmer father of yours ever molested
you with those great callused hands
you, the moon-eyed child
if he penetrated that little white bum of yours
with one of those gigantic fingers of his
swollen from work
or worse
if, if, if . . .
we both know there's nothing I can do but hold you
so that at least you have the strength
to rush to your desk in the morning
and write
and write

2. is the world your father?
is that why it won't let you loose?
I know that tonight I will spend another evening listening to you
list all the evils of the world
— a world I have spent so much time avoiding —
"just don't look," I say
you cannot turn away
as if the world might melt under your gaze
instead it just gets worse
every day there is another
schoolmaster, doctor, lawyer, politician,
censor, fat businessman, or brutal gendarme
the only answer is too fuck them all

I'm so glad that you're trying
but we both know that
their cocks will not save them or us
this only fuels the enthusiasm of our campaign
at least when they're sighing, coming,
or rolled over in a satisfied sleep,
they haven't the strength to kill children, or love
or joy

3. today is one of those days
when I wonder why I stay
my fat pregnant wife loves me much more than you do
and she's much less trouble
then I remember the tender bulge of your scrotum
and the two heavy balls that gently pull at the skin
and my tongue there
your young cock
as it grows unselfconsciously
from slight to weighty in my hands
everything about you is always growing

4. and of course, when you show me a poem
it's all I can do to contain myself
never before have I so enjoyed being surpassed
how is it that a replica of my own unique (and obscene)
consciousness was transplanted into the brain of a farmboy
who then grew up to be my lover?
of course nothing can match the illusion, the fancy
that we may think exactly alike
that we see every tree, every lamb, every injustice
in the same way
there is only one way to find out:
I've made a pact with God, if I
kiss the young beard that grows
just beyond your blushing cheek
one hundred times tonight
God might just let me climb behind your eyes

5. for if I were you
I would walk as proudly as you do
I would break up stately meetings of venerable scholars
with aromatic farts
I would chase reluctant boys when drunk
until they cried "stop!" or begged
me to lay beside them forever
if I were you,
I would be no less beautiful
or less complicated
I would be as gentle and as terrifying as the world

Depressed at Dingwall

There I am, surrounded by tragic luxury:
the sumptuous bad art and purple curtains,
the wallpaper delicately decorated with ribbons of blue,
couches fat and sad, like me,
mirroring my desolation.
I had thoughtlessly left the pornography
running in the bedroom
and soon the mango scented bath overflowed,
there was a dead hooker seated in the kitchen,
his face like a flower collapsed
into a pile of coke,
and another boy was knocking at the door.
"At least I thought he was dead," I said
as I yanked the broad brocade belt of the bathrobe
around my furry middle.
"Oh no, Joe always does that."
The boy's sweet narcolepsy reminded me so much
of that Gus Van Sant film
that I just had to snort some poppers
and fuck him again, while
the second boy watched.
Afterwards I read the conscious
boy a Shakespearean Sonnet
(on constancy)
and we ate
fried bread and strawberries
out of the sleeping
boy's asshole,
dripping with chocolate.
Of course there will always be
boys, bad art, brocade, Shakespeare, and dessert.
But sometimes the unread books
and unplayed piano
simply shriek — "Have a party!"

And so I do.

Soon the glasses are clinking
while the faghags titter,
for the proximity of so many possibly
AIDS infected dicks holds promise of a certain
dangerous excitement.
And yet at dawn, I wake
and it is far too early
to begin the debauch again, and I am
depressed at Dingwall.

FAIRY TALES

I Have Been to Fairyland

I have been to the land of the fairies
I find their dances very charming
and there is something about their wings
so carefully glued on
I have observed their antique rituals
the annointing with precious oils
and the bowing down
of slave before queen
I have been invited
to their fairy parties
to the much heralded gatherings
in vaulted arbors
and the fireflies have kissed my skin
weaving threads of heavenly light
I have witnessed the rush, at dawn
as the fairies scurry to their woodland homes
lest the sunlight
dampen their fairy dreams
indeed, I have spent countless veiled hours
enchanted within their spells
and still I would have you lift your hand
from the table
I would observe the thinness of your neck
I would have you touch me in that slow,
careful way
yes, I have been to fairyland
I have watched their golden feathered gowns
burned to dust by approaching day
yes, I have seen the fairies
and I have also turned away

Ode to Carol Marcus

here's to Carol Marcus, this century's premiere waif
and I bet you've never even heard of her
she was William Saroyan's wife (twice)
and the model (purported)
for Truman's Holly
then she married Walter Matthau
and has not been heard of since
imagine my surprise
to come across her in Kenneth Tynan's diaries
oh yes, she fucked him too
and sucked him, and was also very pleasantly spanked
several times, by his long, elegant, British hands
we love you Carol Marcus
you are everything a muse should be
sexually aggressive, with a little girl voice
and you didn't even care

since we're not liable to ever meet, this is my postcard

dear Carol,
having a wonderful time
but it wouldn't be half as wonderful without you
those guys thought they made you do it
but you made them do it to you
ice cream wouldn't melt in your mouth
and the eiderdown of your smile is not
half as sweet as your mad kneecaps
which unequivocally point towards heaven
I'll pet a dog for you
and plant a snicker
I'll bet you anything
it grows

Our Joy Was Cruel

Michael had finally been confronted
at The Second Cup
so we were feeling very gay
and cruel
in a Christmassy sort of way
and I swept you in my arms
it was a Christmas card, really
and the windows were Hudson's Bay
I finally said "I love you"
and then you said it too
over and over again until you couldn't stop
and for one mad moment we forgot that we were homosexuals
and kissed in front of the atrociously decorated
holiday windows
families stopped beside us
and then hurt by our love
they hurried their strollers away
shielding the tender eyes of their children
I was embarrassed
"but we're family too!" you said
a little ironically
which is, of course, why I love you
we couldn't kiss there any longer
it seemed too much like child abuse
so I dragged you behind the building
to Ruttle Street
and we kissed again
this time no longer furtive
in front of the Barbie windows
thank God, no one saw us there
except for one little boy
a stray
in a yellow muffler and red shoes
for a moment, he stopped and stared

at the big bald man kissing
the slender pretty one
and then he scurried away
we hoped
to ask Santa for that Fashion Barbie

Apartment Hunting

We had thought that we were normal —
that is, when we walked in the door
we supposed that no one could see
our perversity on us.
In our minds we were the perfect couple;
romantic, even.
I, the taller one, distinguished.
You the diffident, elegant boy.
How were we to know that our strangeness
was evident, and that she could barely
contain her disgust?
How were we to know?
Like an old man who passes by a mirror
and is surprised
we were caught off guard.
Only seconds after meeting us, the landlady
saw you, kneeling on the bed, fellating me.
Or she saw even worse,
yes even worse things.
She saw me licking your ass
and she saw the devil too,
children born fine and innocent, who
once giggled and played in fields of hay,
roasted in ovens of infernal design.
Yes, she saw us gnawing on their tasty bones
and she saw me wipe the dripping baby fat
from your cheek before gingerly passing
an infant's tender eyeball from between my teeth
into your eager, salivating mouth.
Yes, the landlady saw it all.
And worse things, things I mustn't say.
We should have worn perfume
to hide the smell of our decay,
we made a grand mistake.

But our crime was only this:
we had thought that we were normal
but she could see that we were us.

Key Largo

call me shallow
or just deeply inattentive
but I'd never seen it before
and when I did, it bored me
Lionel Barrymore is such a lousy actor
Lauren Bacall's hair is practically in a bun
and she's not even being a bit naughty
Humphrey Bogart's integrity and bravery
are yet again in question
and at some point, it all seems to be about patriotism
Edward G. Robinson perks things up a bit though
and then Claire Trevor appears
a drunken woman who certainly has possibilities
she turns out to be Edward G.'s rapidly aging girlfriend
an alcoholic, ex-cabaret singer
well, now we're cooking with gas
her name is "Gay Dawn"
(could anything be more homosexual?)
and she's always drunk
and prone to melodramatic outbursts

The best scene is where she's desperate for a drink and Edward G. won't give her one because, after all, there's a hurricane raging, and it's broken most of the liquor bottles. But Gay just must have her scotch. Edward G. says, "Sing us a song — you know, the old one you used to sing, about men hurtin' you."

And Gay says, "No, I don't want to sing,"

Then Edward G. says, "Come on, sing it like you used to."

And Gay gets an idea: "If I sing that song, will you give me a drink?"

"Sure," says Edward G. So Gay proceeds to sing "Moaning Low," perhaps the most masochistic torch song every written, without accompaniment — *a capelly*, as they used to say.

And when she's done she grabs Edward G.'s sleeve and tugs

desperately, pleading, "Can I have that drink now, Johnny?"

He looks at her as if she's a piece of moldy cheese and says, "Nah."

"But Johnny, you promised if I sang that song, you'd give me a drink."

"I know."

"So honey why can't I have one?"

"Because you sang it lousy," says the merciless Edward G.

Now, there's a lesson to be learned here, and it's much more important than what can be gleaned from Humphrey Bogart's silly, tortured, ex-war hero vacillations over whether or not to protect Lauren Bacall's honour.

And the lesson is this: if you don't sing the song well, then you might not get that drink. Which is relevant even today. I mean, the last thing a guy wants to to do is listen to a song about how abusive he is, sung badly, by his own bitch.

You know what I mean, don't you, baby?

I woke up only to find myself staring at Nigel's briefs which he had so carelessly tossed on the floor the night before. The sunlight pierced through the dormer window falling on Nigel's shoulder, which was dangling charmingly over the corner of the futon. I could see the blond down on his arm. Suddenly and mercilessly, I wanted to take him there, kiss him, have my way with our youthful limbs at play. I never again wanted to feel regret. Except, regretfully, for that moment last night in the café in Hammersmith when we caught sight of those two old queens gossiping in the corner. Oh, how thankful we were not to be like them. "There, but for the grace of God," Nigel said, "go we!" And we thanked our lucky stars that we would never be old, like them. And they were wearing leather. And we thought to ourselves, there's a blast from the past. Old chatty leather queens. We will never be like them. And we felt safe. Safe from all the ugliness, all the disease, all the effeminacy. Because Nigel is a runner and so am I, and he has a thatched cottage, and both of us are fundamentally male, in the ways that are important, and not kinky either. And then Nigel made me breakfast in that quirky way he has. And I watched his bum wiggle, and I thought how happy we were now to be men who love other men, and don't do drugs (except for "k"), and have well paying jobs during the day. (Not like the old days, the bad old sad old gay old days. Not like that again, never, please, never. No, don't let us be like that, ever. We'd do anything not to be like those who cackle and plead, down on their knees. Please dear God, deliver us from temptation — and what may clearly be our fate. Please.) Sunlight. Breakfast. Nigel's bum. I won't think about it now. After all tomorrow is another . . .

Czech Funeral

The women are all short, their severe blunt cuts dyed blonde
and the men are tall and rangy
with fierce noses and dark beards
their hair pulled back in tight knots
at the back of their strong necks.
I wait of course for the son,
who marches, elegant and beautiful, just behind the coffin.
The priest's belly makes me mad,
he knows he's got us here, listening,
even disbelievers,
so he reads from the execrable St. Paul
and makes us kneel until our calves turn blue.
And then the best friend rises and says the Eulogy —
"He was my friend. We did not have, even, to speak,
to each know what the other was thinking."
Suddenly I spy Sigourny Weaver in the audience —
why would she come to poor George's funeral?
I am not fond of her acting,
but I know she's had a strong lesbian following
and certainly a gay one,
ever since she stood up for the gorillas —
"Get off my mountain!" she raged, her eyes gleaming.
Okay, I'm glad Sigourny came.
But why didn't they realize that George was so much
more than this pederastical priest,
better than the microphones at St. Simon's,
better than the constant reminders of original sin,
better than the pro-life poster in the lobby,
better even, than the little girl with the Sailor Moon backpack,
whose parents urge her to take communion
over the body of a man she barely knew.
The music is thrilling. Some Gounod, and Elgar
and real violins.
I want to get up and scream: "Of course the music is thrilling!

Don't you realize? Wherever there is music there is God!
God is *in the music*, the music is not *in* God!"
But out of respect for Margaret, his tiny perfect wife,
I say nothing.
After all, she phoned me only yesterday.
"I know you didn't really know him, but my husband —"
and there was a catch in her voice, "he died."
Then she said,
"He worked until the very end."
His last name was unpronounceable,
and he could deliver ESP messages to his best friend.
I would love to fuck his son. His wife
is absolutely the nicest person I have ever met.
And still the paunchy priest berates them all
and prattles on about St. Paul.
"George was baptized" the priest says,
over and over again. As if George is so terribly lucky
to be going to heaven.
Yes. He was Czech.
He was a man who worked until the very end.

Roman Holiday

when Audrey Hepburn gets her haircut in
Roman Holiday
it's my whole life really
I mean it looks all droopy at first and like an adolescent
and then the mustachioed barber
(imagine, a princess at a barber!)
poises the scissors
and she says
"cut more"
"like this?" he asks
"no, more"
and indeed at one point we must all cut our hair
it is important of course that it always end up
in a divine little French bob
that perfectly complements our magnificent and saucy smile
and when the barber asks us for a date it is our finest moment
we lower our lashes (and of course our innocent eyes)
"I think . . . not"
after all, Gregory Peck is waiting
or at least he'd better be

TO THE ONE I LOVE

Request

let me kiss the cobwebs from your eyes
my dusty, dusky boy
let me clear the dandruff from your hair
let me be your long forgotten
let me be your never used
tossed aside and woebegotten
let me be your left behind
what you trip over late at night
and rub on your eyelids
let me be your balm
your Gilead and tongs
let me be the piano
in empty rooms where perverts feast
and if we don't see them
it won't matter
let me be your argument
or better yet, your reconciliation
let me be your bath
your bum
your lack of sexual discrimination
the hair on your ears
all spaces beneath and between your thighs
oh, let me clean your kitchen
there is nothing sexier than the lack of time you have
to attend to household chores
let me be your smile
and the easy swing of your walk
let me be what it is that makes you hurry
but especially what makes you slow down
just in case you go away
I'll leave a bit of my self behind the stair
if you turn quickly
you'll almost see me there

("in quotes and parentheses")

I was going to say something really stupid
like "there's summer behind his eyes"
but that just seems too corny
then on the other hand
I was walking down the street
and I had to wait for this light
and it was very cold
and I thought "gee whiz it doesn't seem so fucking cold this winter"
and I couldn't figure out why
and then it occurred to me
in the form of a thought bubble
"hey it's because of him, because I'm around him all the time now"
which doesn't seem possible
and yet it is
it's definitely warmer
(and it's not just because he likes the thermostat turned up
no, it's not just that)
it always seems like summer inside our apartment anyway
(and one of our walls is ice blue
so it has nothing to do with the colour)
I could say something nutty like
"life is less bleak when you're around"
but that's almost barely a compliment
or "I feel much less hopeless around the edges"
or "my ragged style seems charming"
or "what I'm lacking seems less evident"
or lots of other stuff which I won't bother to say here
in fact I'm not sure why I'm quoting myself
(except that I seem more "quotable" these days, too)

Bengali Tea

tell me of your infidelities
in narcotic detail
reveal their every pimple and fold
smell their clothes
deny them every privacy
I want to look at every John and Jeff
at every Joe and Paul
up close
where the truth lives
of course please be especially careful
to linger on what makes them special
on the things you do with them
that you've never done with me
detail the gaps they fill
the places where my sense of humour is guarded, old fashioned
don't say, "we only slept together once"
say, "we slept together a thousand times!
thousands and thousands more times than I've ever had sex
with you! and it wasn't just sex or 'sleeping together!'
it was fucking and rutting and sniffing and poking
plowing and shoving and prodding and stroking
it was rough and tumble, griff and grim!"
say it all
say everything
and so will I
and if we're still alive and breathing
then we can have Bengali tea
and laugh together knowingly
for we have faced an exotic death
in foreign lands
and lived to tell the ordinary tale

As I Am Old and Lame

as I am old and lame
and speak too much
shambled and ambled am I
with neurosis
and you are young and clear
it seems to me
but my eyes are cloudy
with desire
don't step into that car with
that old man!
as if you ever would, really
(troubled, you enter my kitchen
radiant and blonde as day
"three old men yelled at me from their cars")
how do I tell you I am envious
for I am old and lame
and none from cars do yell at me
rather they drive by
quick with fury and fear
o, to be afraid to walk down the street!
but I'll leave that to you
and I will take you in my lame old arms
and hug their lechery away
because with such hugging
my own lechery becomes lechery no more
suddenly it's love

He Should Be as a Bar or Tavern Is

He should be as a bar or tavern is,
your special boy.
And by that I do not mean his length or breadth
or the height of his vaulted ceilings
or his sturdy beams and well-worn floor
or what the wallpaper is concealing.
And I don't mean
the number of times they have broken in,
those pious expungers of delicious sin,
and battered him beyond recognition.
I mean that he should be like your local
watering hole.
There are nights
when you would rather not be there,
when you would, in fact, rather be anywhere else,
and you can't imagine why you picked this particular
hole to drink yourself to death in.
And when you look around you see the crumbling walls
and the drooling, doltish patrons
— there is no joy there
and you can't imagine how there ever, ever was.
(This, your very own favorite bar.)
And yet on other blessed nights
(and who can say why they are so blessed?)
that self-same bar is the very distillation
of a clean, dim place —
it is mother, father, sister, brother,
and it is here that you are safe.
And you would like to hug the lights
or swing unabashedly from them,
as you would like to kiss his eyes
and dance each fevered dance
with every desperate boy
until the darkness dies.

Choose one like that.
One who like a bar or tavern is.
For it is to him
you will find yourself
returning
again and again and again.

Ruminations

You fixed the snapflap on my leather jacket
when we were walking down the stairs;
it was completely instinctive and maternal
and it made me fall in love with you
for the thousandth time. Do you think that's bad?
that I constantly, you know, put you into
movie images in my mind, images that
are not real but are in a certain way still
you. That is — I'm not expressing myself right —
it seemed to happen all of a sudden and to be
natural and real. As if you were a boy who
loved me, all of a sudden.

Limping down the street the other day
with arthritis, which pains me and makes me old,
I noticed people ignoring me or just being
irritated by my slowness. Then I thought of
the mask of wrinkles that was growing over
my real face, and how it would make people
forget about me, except to be annoyed.
At first, terror; and then — well, it's a kind of
disguise. Ian talks to me about being in
a bathhouse and ten hairy old wrinkly hands
grabbing at him through a glory hole,
desperate for the feel of young flesh. Will
that be me? I think not. We become
what we have been before, only more so.
But I'm looking forward to my disguise
and spying on the young through wintry
spectacles of bluish veined glass.

There are two anticipations, and they
both involve stairs. One is you walking up
mine. As Christopher once said: Does your

heart beat faster when he climbs the stairs? Why
yes it does. And then there's visiting Towers
classical record shop, which is on the second
floor. I usually take the elevator, but there's still the
anticipation. That the boys working there will
be rude, and Pachelbel's Canon or Barber's
Adagio will be playing. But there's also the calm. I mean,
knowing that there are so many great composers
to discover one at a time, and each little
jewel box sparkles and twinkles when
you hold it up to the light. There will be much
joy. And anticipating it. As when I'm thinking,
what will he say? Will he run into my arms
or will he be sulking? Either one, my beautiful
boy, I'll take either one.

My Love Is Like a New England Town

my love is like a New England town
there is a solitary oyster shop down by the bay
it's closed in winter
Nathaniel Hawthorne slept here
the doors are closed, but the lights are on
you can see them twinkling through the windows
no one goes to church anymore, except the old ladies
but the steeple is lovely
you can see it for miles around

And once every year they pick a girl to be "Hester". They strip her naked and paint her with an "A". It's fun for Hester because she gets to be humiliated in ways she never even imagined. She rolls around in the dirt and screams for "Daddy". Hester yells, "Daddy! Piss on me! Please!"

The townsfolk cheer her degradation.
They throw rocks that always miss.
And afterwards, they go home
and yank their curtains shut and fuck
like they just saw *The Rocky Horror Picture Show.*

my love is like a New England town
as lovely and intemperate
lashing and sulking with a torpid morbidity
as changeable as the sea
and as calm as a clam
to me, he smells like redemption

FROM "WHAT LITTLE TRUTHS WE KNOW FOR SURE ABOUT THE LIFE AND TIMES OF CASPER G. SCHMIDT"

What Casper G. Schmidt Did Every Night Before Going to Bed

every night before going to bed Casper G. Schmidt
would lay out his clothes for the next morning
the blue seersucker in May
or on a crisp autumn night
the brown tweed jacket might lay poised
over the Louis the 16th chair in his closet
sometimes the sight of his own clothes
so displayed
would cause this sensitive man to weep
(which Casper did almost silently
into his tender, slender fingers)
for the clothes held within them
sweet expectation

Casper told no one
about his tears
and if young Manny happened to notice his wet lapels
Casper would wink and say
"it vas rainink!"
young Manny forgave the lie
because of the possibility of love
which hovered over all their meetings
like a bird
or an insect
or (and I know you won't believe me)
a fairy

Though Casper G. Schmidt Is Dead He Still Lives On

Casper G. Schmidt still moves about his rooms
he still lights a fire
on Wednesday nights he still takes young Manny
to the Café Lalo
and shares a torte with him
he still ponders, challenges, considers and confronts
all the hatred in the world

Casper G. Schmidt still masturbates
and thinks of young Manny
and afterwards shares a cigarette with himself
and stares down 83rd Street
imagining he can see Central Park
from his elegant second floor balcony

though he only sees
the very tops of the trees
sometimes
that really is enough

Why Casper G. Schmidt Wrote Tiny Elegant Books

Casper G. Schmidt inscribed hundreds
of tiny elegant books
on fragile parchment
with the most painstaking calligraphic hand
because wisdom is small
and the most important things in the world
can be held in one hand
if they can be "held" at all
on some pages there is nothing
and that is important too

"If it doesn't fit into a tiny book"
Casper once said
"then it's barely worth knowing"

Casper suggested that thoughts should be tiny too
and beautiful
they should make you laugh
quietly
afterwards
like a lover's dolphin smile

WORLD WEARY

My Throat Hurts

I've never had sex on the train before and now my throat hurts. It could be Jo-Jo stabbing at it with his nine-inch cock or it could be the cold (we're just passing through Virginia). I feel sorry for Jody but he sure was hard to resist. Right off he plops himself down opposite me in the smoking car and says, "I'm just a country boy from South Carolina," and then starts to peel up his shirt and show off his shaved tummy. Then there was the heavily made up woman's eyes tattooed on his head (that he was so proud of) that made it look — when he was sucking you off — like a pretty lady was doing it. Then there was the bloody tattoo around his neck that made it look like his head had been cut off and resewn on again. Then there was the way he said, "That's cause my daddy used to tell me as a kid I was so crazy that my head was gonna fly off, so I decided to have it sewn on permanently." My own worry about the regret I may have in the future over the anchor tattooed on my forearm pales. Everything pales, actually, though I keep reminding myself that Jo-Jo is a crazy 24 year old who sets up video stores in different cities before getting the hell out of town. And he's living off mommy's credit card right now, and he sure seems vulnerable and lonely (he demanded I fall asleep with him in his coach seat later, but this time no funny business because the conductor was onto us), whereas I'm a PhD student and a writer with a lover. But all that means absolutely nothing when Jo-Jo grabs me and we run to the back of the train, the very back of the last car, and he whispers, "See, there's no one here darlin'! We can have all the fun we want!" And suffice it to say we do. I feel bad that I can't get hard though, and that's because part of me (obviously the wrong part) is already having breakfast the following morning in the dining car, with people who remind me very much of my parents. They seem very nice, but it upsets me that they wouldn't understand me sucking off Jo-Jo in the back of the train or how we moved into the washroom for privacy and so I could get a better view of his dick. No, I don't think they would understand.

Am I two people? I can certainly answer the question, "Do you like suckin' on that big country boy's dick, darlin'?" as easily as, "Are you afraid you'll arrive late for your appointment in New York City?" The first answer is yes and the second is yes I am afraid.

Key West Notes

1. The musak in the guesthouse is now murdering "Moon River." Contrary to popular belief, you can kill "Moon River" (Liberace did it, too). Usually the guesthouse plays something called "new age" which is basically Debussy on drugs — lots of tinkling, no moonlight. There was also "Mack the Knife" played murderously slow. Once, when I was telling one of my classes what's wrong with Brecht I mentioned that the song we all love to hum is actually about a serial killer. I don't think anyone heard me.

2. A fat, middle-aged businessman from Milwaukee or someplace is sitting in a lounge chair with a six-toed cat on his lap, petting it as it purrs contentedly. Those cats are rife with fleas and disease, but I'm certainly not going to tell him.

3. The fags, as usual, pointedly ignore me. (Now, of course, I understand this is the gay way of saying "I want you.") The homeless and the drug addicted, however, are extra responsive. As I lurched home from a porn video store last night a stoned homeless guy stood bolt upright and yelled, "Wow!" Because I have, approximately, the emotional maturity of a thirteen year old, I was complimented. He took it back, though. "Nah, he hasn't got muscles, he's just big." I flirted momentarily with being hurt, until realizing that a) it was true, and b) I had just been insulted by someone who a lack of food and a plethora of drugs had probably driven out of his mind. Almost immediately I felt guilty about my second presumption.

4. Race has a way of intruding into everything in America. That is, unless you can ignore the fact that everyone serving you is black. I still find this disconcerting. My guest house, for instance, lies at the edge of the black section of Key West, an area we have been directed, in no uncertain terms, never to enter. And the guesthouse is surrounded by an eight-foot-high wooden fence.

Of course, I have never seen a black gay man staying here, at our "all-male, clothing-optional compound." So is it odd that someone jumped over the fence last night and broke the jacuzzi? And is it racist for me to assume it was one of the blacks from the surrounding village? But wouldn't that make sense? "We'll fix those rich fucking faggots. We'll break their jacuzzi. They won't be able to fuck each other without a jacuzzi. That's where they pick each other up, you know."

5. Since I have been coming here for over ten years now, I now know what happens to pool boys. They become older pool boys. In every other respect, they remain the same.

6. Ron, the owner of this guesthouse, has also remained the same. Except he has not aged. I don't expect he ever will. Perpetually dapper and flawlessly handsome, a cocktail and cigarette always in hand, he bustles about his domain whispering droll directives to his staff with the air of a benevolent despot, a preoccupied schoolmarm. The last time I was here he was nursing an ailing and very beautiful boy, whom he obviously outlived. He will, doubtless, outlive them all.

7. I haven't been here for five years, and gaytown has changed. Like everything, it has become gentrified. There used to be two watering holes: an upscale dance club and an all-purpose bar. The all-purpose bar was my favorite. I remember once seeing a very slender, elderly gay man there with something packed into his pants. It was either a dead baby or a penis and balls of such grotesque proportions that any doctor would certainly have classified him as deformed. Now there are several bars, which, like cars, cater to each person's particular fantasy. There is a drag bar, a strip bar, a leather bar, and a video bar for rich boys. There is no longer an all-purpose bar. You must decide what you want to be, pick the appropriate bar, and hang out there in search of others of your ilk. My ilk, however, remains in perpetual flux.

8. I was perturbed when a young man sucking my cock and pulling my balls (I was close to coming) said, "That's it, go for it Daddy, yeah!" Daddy? What was that? Did I miss something? Daddy? Well, I suppose I must learn to accept it. (When I say young, I mean that he was considerably younger than I am — he may well have been thirty-five.)

9. Everyone here, when they go out at night, wears whatever clothing and hairdo was a magnificent, lucky hit in their home town. Thus you are treated to the disconcerting sight of badly dyed platinum blond, rapidly aging boyettes from Ohio sporting fabulous mesh t-shirts that are cut just short enough to reveal their unappealing bellybuttons. I am no different, of course, and dress in my heartwenching black shorts and black string tank top. I'm confounded because no one tries to pick me up. Not surprisingly, middle-aged wrestlers are even less popular here than they are in Toronto.

10. But still. A fat man is rolling his suitcase out of the guest house, after a vacation that was, I'm sure, far too short. He carries a pathetic yellow gift bag with "Key Lime Gift Shoppe" written on it in old fashioned letters. He gazes around himself hopefully, but no one recognizes him or bothers to say goodbye. They do more than ignore him (that would be flirting); he is simply not there. But is there not a kind of transcendence in invisibility? If so, will someone please tell him? After all, you can slip in and out of the tightest places. I know I can, and do.

Why You're Not Like All Those Other Guys

1. Some of them have protease-inhibitor faces. I mean, if they wanted to mark us for life they couldn't have found a better way. If they wanted, for future reference, to figure out which ones were us by feeding us disfiguring drugs which made us all look the same, they couldn't have done it more efficiently, could they? I mean, last night I was having sex with one and all the time I was trying to figure out what he used to look like, before the lines around the mouth and the shrunken cheeks. It's a fantasy I use now to get off when I'm with one of them, imagining what they might have looked like, before.

But I don't have to use that fantasy with you.

2. I will never completely possess you (*Proust*).

3. Last night I heard a couple of them talking after they picked up a trick together. "He didn't like me," the older one said.

"Why do you say that?" the younger, skinnier, blonde one with the horrible mustache who earlier was going on and on about how large the pool was in their fabulous place in Fort Lauderdale so loud that everyone in the guesthouse could hear, said.

"He just didn't like me, that's all, I heard him say it."

"I never heard him say that."

"He did."

"Well I didn't hear him."

"Well he did. It doesn't matter," the older one who was actually much beautifuller than the younger incredibly evil one, said.

"Oh well, I'm sorry. I didn't hear him say that."

Then the younger unbelievably evil one went inside to change into one of his thousand and one bathing suits and didn't come out for ages, so the older one (who really was more beautiful than the younger one, even though I know it's hard to believe) just sat there in silence looking very sad.

We would never have a conversation like that.

4. You will understand this piece of writing, and it might even make you smile.

5. None of them will stand in my room slightly self-consciously, not wearing a shirt, with your young muscles gleaming in the moonlight, shivering, because my room is always too cold for you, and say, "My stomach is too big."

6. For some of them — when they have sex — it's not like they're opening a wonderful gift and enjoying it with you. It's as if they don't enjoy sharing the gift of pleasure. They tease you and then go away or they act like something was missing, or like they want to get it over with because it's something bad (and besides, you weren't really good enough), or they have something you don't. (Like real attractiveness.)

It's not like that with you.

7. Some of them only share their experiences in a competitive way.

8. Some of them talk about computer programmers, or their work with the military, or farm implements.

9. There's no light there.

There's just no light.

10. And of course, this goes without saying.

I don't love them.

Montreal Morning

perhaps it's the perfectly toasted bagel
the exquisitely crumbled cream cheese
and the delicately fried potatoes
that melt in my mouth
or the waiter
an impossibly beautiful youth
who actually apologizes
for not knowing English
or the memory of that boy
from last night
with the long, everhard cock
who so carefully removed his glasses
before pressing me onto the bed
and forcing me to look at myself in the mirror
"You like this big hard cock
inside you?" he asked
(rhetorically)
perhaps it's the sunlight
or the cross on the mountain
or the fact that
boys still try to talk
like porn stars
but for some reason
I'm crying

When Some Old Ladies

when some old ladies talk to you
it's as if they know
or knew
or remember
like the maid in my hotel who
sees me stagger out of my room
at 10:30 a.m.
"morning" she says and it holds
all the muted, generous understanding
of love and sex and hey I'm a big guy
and somewhere she appreciates my body
and the fact that I've been throwing it
around the city the night before
you know, the way some people do
unlike other old ladies
for instance Phyllis Grosskurth
biographer of Byron
who treats me
with a kind of chilly warmth
with all the sweetness of a winter's day
her huge green spectacles
falling off her left ear
I realize, on close inspection
that she is incredibly old
but that doesn't matter
I mean you don't forget about sex
the maid in my hotel remembered
probably smelled my sheets
in search of tell-tale signs of love
but not finding it, thought
he got it somewhere out on the town
and smiling to herself
didn't bother to change the bed

I want to be an old lady
who remembers
the rough and tussle
the scratchy feel of
hay on my back
of sand between my toes
of love on the run
of the joy
of desperate hurried longing
quickly spent

The Most Beautiful Houseboy in the World

And I've stayed in a lot of bed and breakfasts. But he's the most beautiful houseboy I've ever seen and somewhere across the way on a balcony I can see two very pretty fags making dinner and playing with the cat. Now they're back in their apartment. They make me think of us. And the two drag queens yelling at each other on the street the other day — "Will you hurry up! You're making us late, girl!" — that too, reminded me of us. The houseboy makes me think of you because you would like him too I think. He's young of course, as they must always be, and dark, and I met him two times — especially once when I came in late and so did he and we were both drunk. And then today when I was trying to write this and he came out on the deck and started to play the guitar. I thought of telling him to stop, and then I thought, he's the most beautiful houseboy I've ever seen. And that's the part of him that reminds me of you. (Besides the fact that he interrupted me when I was working which you always do.) Because it's like I've seen a lot of houseboys (as I said, I have) but not one of them measures up to you. And there are times when I think I might ask you to stop playing the guitar (and by guitar I mean loving me), but then I figure no, you play guitar much better than the most beautiful houseboy in the world — if I haven't taken the metaphor too far. And I know you will be offended by being called a houseboy, especially because you never clean house and it feeds into that whole older/younger thing. You're not my houseboy and you never will be, but can't I just have my fantasy? Which is related to reality, mainly because it keeps cropping up. Anyway, I was sitting out on this stupid balcony of this stupid bar this afternoon and all the stupid faggots just kept walking by (a lot of them were on Protease Inhibitors I could tell, and it made me think of you and how angry the medical establishment can make you) and then I started to cry for no reason. And it was probably all the stress just floating away because I am on vacation. But I don't think so. I think I just realized that I am inextricably linked to you, so to say that I miss you is ultimately stupid and a waste of time. I don't miss you at all. Just now and then I start crying and then I think to myself, he's home. He's just sitting at home. He'll be there when you get back. And unlike the most beautiful houseboy in the world he's not cleaning, or playing guitar badly, or even coming home drunk. He's littering the apartment with Kraft dinner boxes and kiwi skins that I'll have to clean up when I get back. That's the part I'm really looking forward to, cleaning up your mess again. Which I guess makes me the houseboy. And at one point last week you did say I looked like a porno picture, remember, when I lifted my arms above my head in a certain way? So I guess that makes us even. What happens when two beautiful houseboys meet? It's a cataclysm, it's a tidal wave, a tornado. And then the house explodes. . . .

Real Life Among the Walking Dead

I'm drunk and it's all shit and I just left Jody Jo-Jo in the smoking room. What can I say, it's all over so why should I continue. But let me mention Stabbie. Stabbie is the guy who got stabbed in South Beach. That is, he's tall and blonde and has a pierced eyebrow and wears sunglasses on his head, and Jo-Jo thinks he's gay but, the thing is, it doesn't matter what he is, it's enough that he got on the train and was still bleeding. (They almost didn't let him on, but then he changed his shirt and it was okay.) Some guy stabbed him and his lung collapsed, so Jo-Jo calls him Stabbie. Stabbie can't really say much about it — except there was a girl involved and the guy was his best friend. "I was on the red light" he says, which means he was almost dead. It was that close to his heart. What is alarming but funny to us is that he is still smoking. And drinking. And having fun and joking. He's the closest to a walking dead person I've ever met, I say. And then another guy tells me he was electrocuted once, and Jo-Jo goes — *no offense, but I can tell from the way you talk, you know, and that look in your eye.* And the guy says none is taken — and it's true the guy does look a little weird. So there's Stabbie and the electrocuted guy and also a really fat stoner girl from California, whose problem is that she hits people — at least that's what she says — that when she starts laughing it gets out of control and she hits people, and injures them sometimes, and she seems to be a lesbian, I'm not sure. And then there's the guy sitting opposite us who's a swinger (24), here with his wife (45), and he's into trains, intensely, scarily into trains, and Jo-Jo tries to sell him a video game. The swinger says that he and his wife had a great time, a great time he says, on the DisneyWorld cruise. Apparently it was too much fun, *so much fun* that they can't even express it — and there seems to have been some swinging involved. So it's nice for me to know that this is real life and the real walking dead are here in the smoking car. And all those ads on TV where the wives are hugging their husbands at DisneyWorld, well, I know what's really going on. Not just

DisneyWorld, but swinging. Though perhaps not stabbings and electrocutions. (Maybe in the future, in the mega-mega-Disney.) And Jo-Jo is still showing photos of his gay cruise and trying to sell video games. And hey, we're not even out of Florida yet.

My Summer Vacation 2000

In Connecticut:
On Monday we went shopping and my Dad tried to get me running shoes instead of boots but I said no. I thought that I had started a pattern of asserting myself. But then on Tuesday morning we went swimming and I took out my nipple ring so as not to upset him. On Tuesday afternoon Lois almost died when she choked on her taco at Chili's. She's seventy-eight. "They started this place in Texas, didn't they?" my father asked. But the waitress didn't know.

In New York City:
I saw a very good movie except the homosexual character hanged himself at the end. (He was naked too. Why do they always have to be naked?) And the straight characters continued with their lives while learning valuable lessons from their friend's tragic, untimely death. The movie made me mad so I decided to go to a drag bar and I met a very hairy Italian named Jeff Buttafuoco, who lived in Jersey. (Why do they always have to live in Jersey?) But he was housesitting in Chelsea, thank God. Oh, and he lived up to his name.

On the train to Toronto:
Right now I have to fill out my customs declaration card. I have decided to declare my genius. I'm going to use this prose as proof. (I decided not to call it poetry because, well, that would be pushing it.) It shouldn't be a problem though, because the dollar value of this poem is nil and you're allowed at least a hundred dollar exemption (Canadian).

DESSERT

Letters to God

1. You do exist and everything don't you? I'm asking for my next door neighbour. No, really, I'd tell you if it was me. He phones me almost every day to just, well, chat. But sometimes he phones me and asks me if you exist. (He's got other problems too, like thinking the phone is tapped, and that he has to wash his hands all the time, but I won't bother you with that now.) For him, it's a big thing. A very big thing. If he knew for sure that you existed then maybe he wouldn't cry so much. And when he asks me if you exist I don't really know what to say. I remember what The Minister said to me when I was ten. He said "Look at the trees. The trees prove there is a God. Every fall they die and in the spring they are born again. This proves that there is a resurrection. And if there is resurrection, there is God." I'm afraid my neighbour is a tad too sophisticated for that. You don't have to tell me you exist. Tell *him*. His phone number is 416-864-0270. Ignore the crazy recorded message (you can push "pound" to skip past it — not many people know this) and just tell him you're around — *if* you have the time.

2. Could you make my boyfriend like my cat? Or at least start saying, "Hey, I'm going to boil up Maggie one day for dinner" with a little less *actual* hatred. Or make it totally a joke. Yeah — make it a joke when he says that.

3. Hi, howya doin'? I was masturbating today and it suddenly occurred to me that the Pope had called Postmodernism the "devil's work." I was just wondering if you agreed with him on this. My feeling is that he's getting a little old (I don't know if you remember, but he collapsed in the middle of some edict last week) and may be a might addled. It also occurred to me that Foucault and Barthes, two very big postmoderns, were raging homosexuals, and the Pope might not like them. It also occurred to me that the Postmodern spin on The Bible might be that it's just a document and not your Word. Actually, you could sure clear

up a lot of shit if you just told me whether or not the Bible is actually your word. I'm sure it's not. I'm sure Peter and Paul got in there and fucked it up. Also (since I've already broached the subject of masturbation), is *any* sexual fantasy okay? Don't ask me why, but I need to know this right away. Or at least soon. Thanks.

4. What about Lilith?

5. Could you make my boyfriend's eyes just a little less crossed? Actually he's not cross-eyed — not at all — he just has this one lazy eye that sort of lists to the centre. Could you put it right? And also, while you're at it, could you cure his parasomnia (that's the technical term for sleepwalking) and also his dyslexia and his recurring strep throat? And what the hell, could you completely eradicate his Wolf-Parkinson-White-Syndrome? It's almost gone anyway, but we really don't want to have to worry that he's going to drop dead from just like one coffee or a cigarette here and there. Also, you might as well clear up his allergy to mangoes. Every time he eats a salad I insist on checking it for him and then we have a fight. Thanks, God. You're a *real* pal. I mean it. I do.

6. How can consciousness think about itself?

7. In the movie *American Beauty* the ex-mental patient son of the crazy homophobic ex-army guy makes a video in which he describes a plastic bag as being the essence of eternal life. Is it the essence of eternal life, or just a plastic bag? If you have to take a lot of time with this one, that's okay. I'm going to New York City next weekend anyway, so I won't be picking up my mail.

8. Whenever I'm really afraid of death, could you just remind me about the fact that I'm one of, like, billions of people who have died? And lots of them have died lonely and in pain and agony. And I'm probably going to die, if not suddenly, then at least with the help of lots of morphine? Could you just help me to realize

that it's incredibly selfish and stupid of me to worry about my inconsequential little death in the face of all that? This is something which I often forget, and I'm sure I'll forget it at the crucial moment, you know, of expiring, so just remind me.

9. Sometimes when I kiss my boyfriend good-bye at the subway, it just seems like he's the most fragile boy in the world, and the wind is whipping around plastic bags (but they're not looking eternal or anything), and the moon is up there, somewhere, and it's like we're Romeo and Juliet or something. I wish I could be more articulate about this. Can you tell me, is our love special at all? Or are there thousands of other people like us, who love in the same way? How can we know, since we can't get inside other people's heads? How, in fact, can we presume to know anything? Wouldn't it be better if we just discovered everything all the time as if it was new, but never actually named it, or analyzed it? Isn't knowledge dangerous, ultimately (the apple), so tell me, how can we remain fools? Why is the ice-cream I like always missing or out of stock and sometimes unheard of? Why does aging have to be so painful? I really hate the stock market and the obsession people have with it — could you make it crash again? Could you make it so that when someone says "I love you" they just have to mean it or they will get struck by lightning? Oh, and bring back Audrey Hepburn.

10. I was wrong about uncrossing my boyfriend's eyes. I like them the way they are. But I guess that's why you decided to leave them that way. Thanks.

How to Take Care of My Cat

1. Don't put her in the oven.
2. Please don't kick her or beat her or pull out her eyes with hot tongs or drop her out the window. And don't take the window-screen off and then accidentally push her out.
3. Don't put that little bottle of mercury you have in her food.
4. Don't let her play with the little bottle of mercury, even if it *is* plastic.
5. Remember that when she bites you, she's just playing. She's not evil and has nothing against you.
6. Feed her at twelve o'clock midnight or when she starts clawing the furniture. Fill one side of her bowl with food.
7. Give her fresh water every morning.
8. I'll take care of the kitty litter box because I love you.
9. If you feel like dangling her Sailor Moon toy for her so she can chase it, go right ahead. If she's antsy, Sailor Moon usually calms her down. But of course you don't have to play with her if you don't want to.
10. Remember I love you much more than I do her. She's not my boyfriend.

She's just a cat.

But of course that's no reason to kill her.

P.S. I'll be back on Thursday evening.
P.P.S. She'll probably miss me and meow a bit. Remember the Sailor Moon toy.
P.P.P.S. I noticed that she was sniffing around that ashtray on the stand that we stole from the lobby, and particularly the sand in it. To her, it probably feels a lot like kitty litter. Anyway, just so that she won't poop in the ashtray on the stand, I put the Barry Manilow program on top of it to protect it. I mean, neither of us likes Barry Manilow, but the word "Barry" looks nice there and we can just take the program off if one of our guests wants to smoke and use the ashtray on a stand. Is that okay?
P.P.P.P.S. I love you.

Sky Gilbert is a writer and theatre director who lives in Hamilton. (He is also an award winning playwright and the founding artistic director of Buddies in Bad Times Theatre in Toronto.) His theatre memoir *Ejaculations from the Charm Factory* was published by ECW in 2000. His first three novels: *Guilty* (1998), *St. Stephen's* (1999), and *I Am Kasper Klotz* (2001) were critically acclaimed. *An English Gentleman*, his fourth novel, was published by Cormorant Books in October, 2003. By day, Sky Gilbert is an assistant professor of Theatre Studies at Guelph University. This is his second collection of poetry.